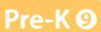

Weather

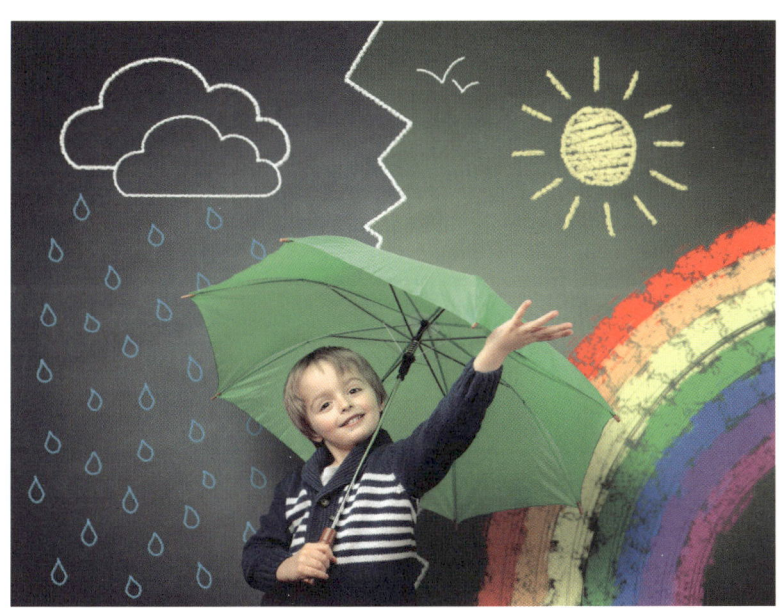

Seed Learning

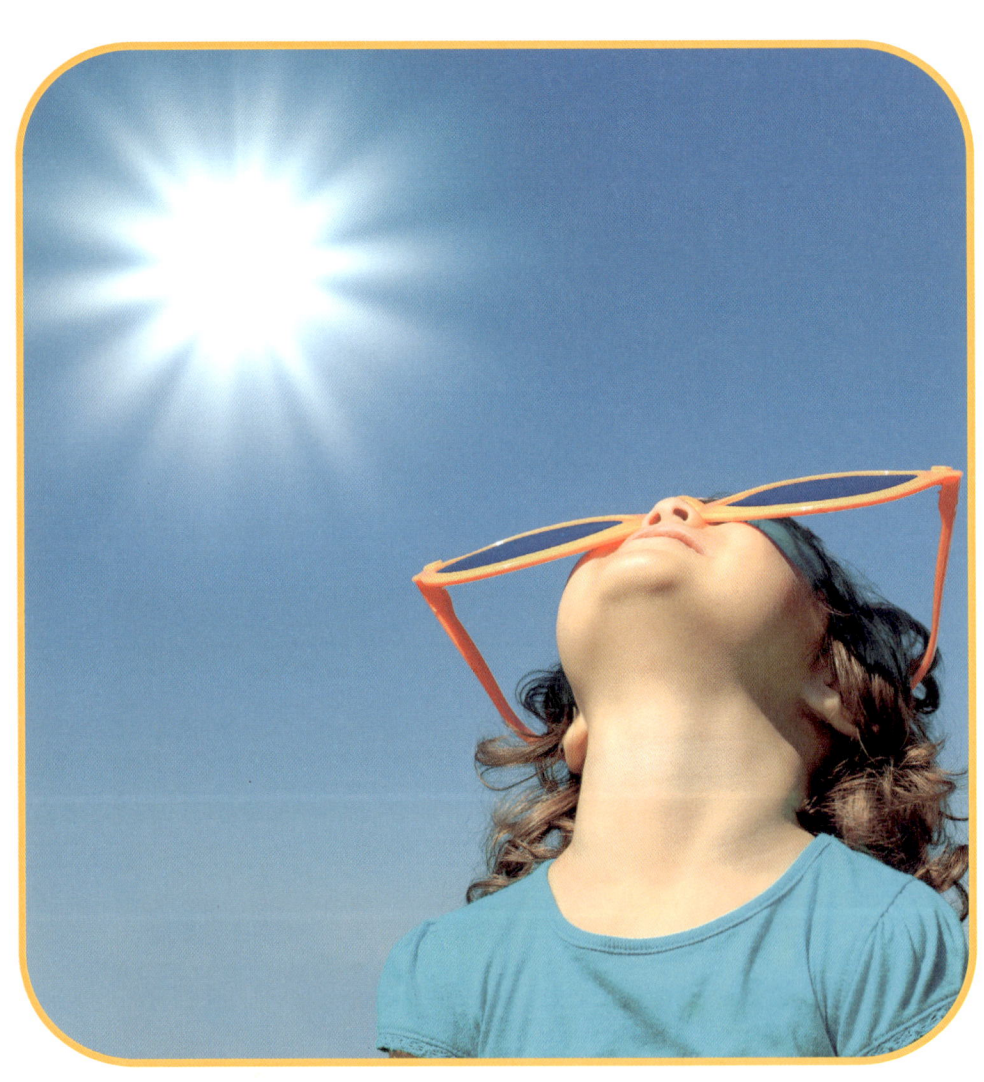

sunny

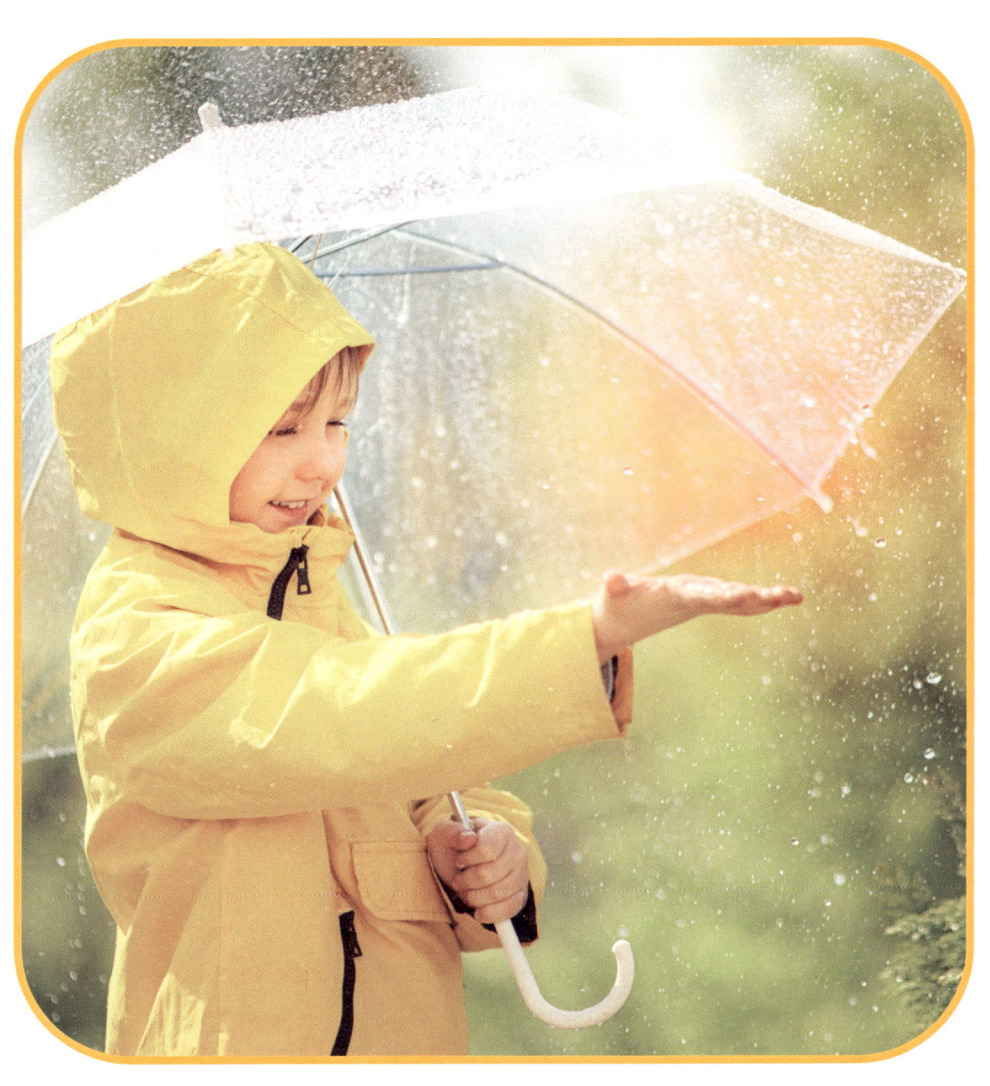

rainy

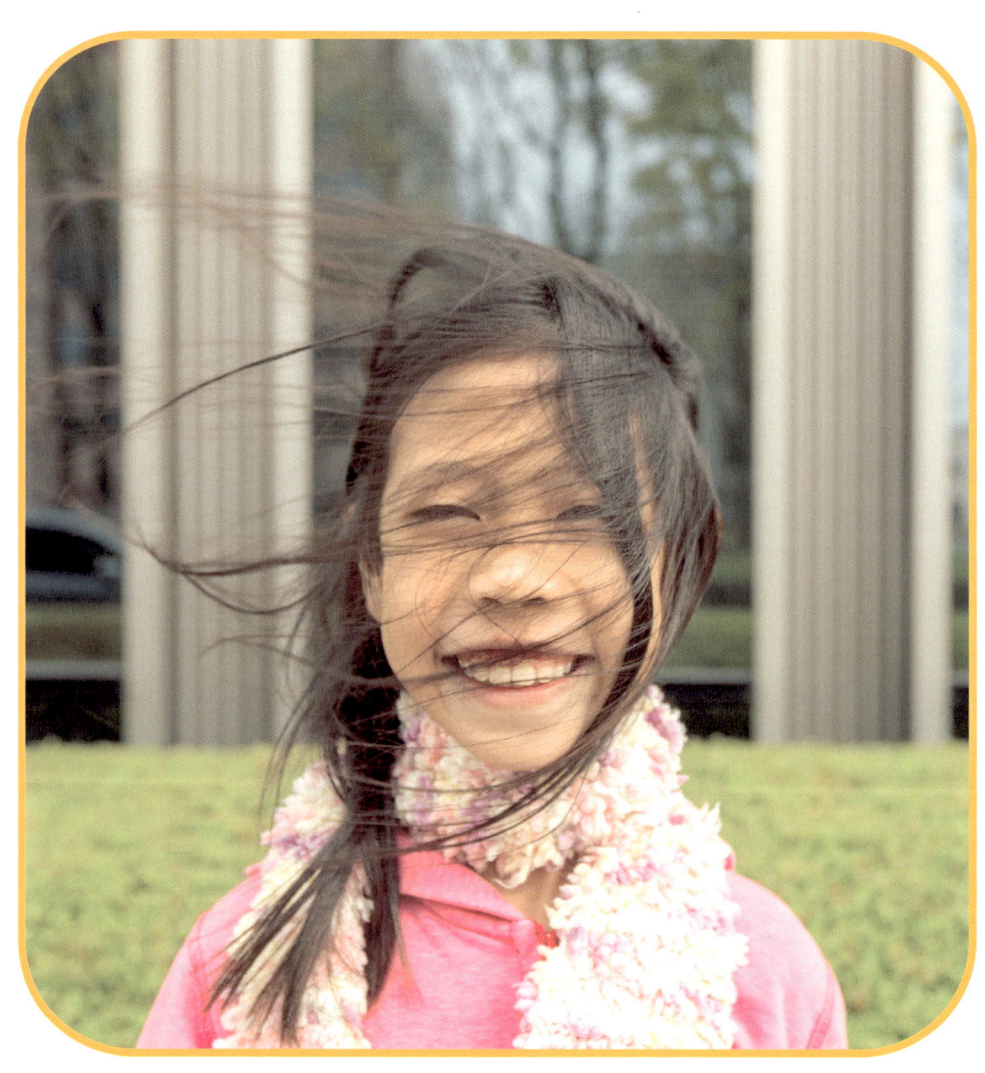

windy

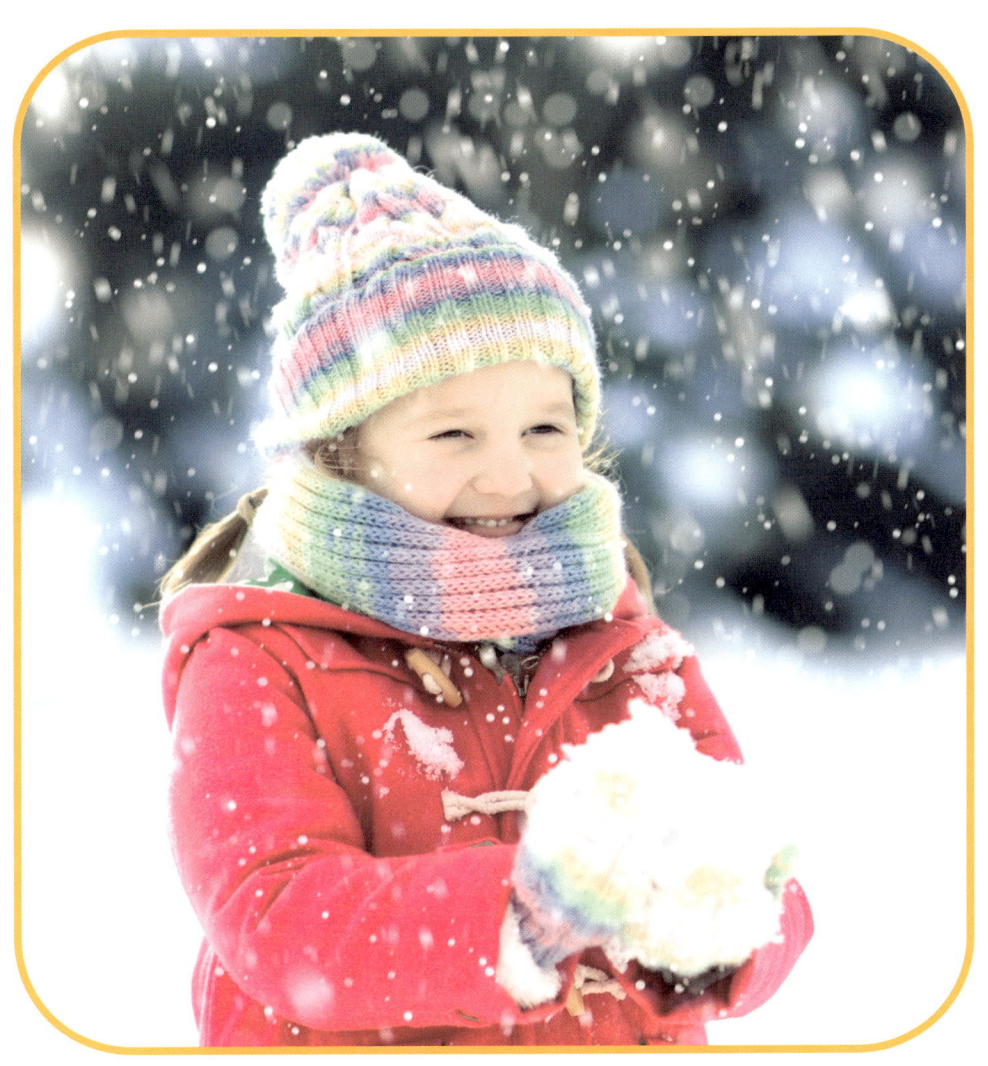

snowy

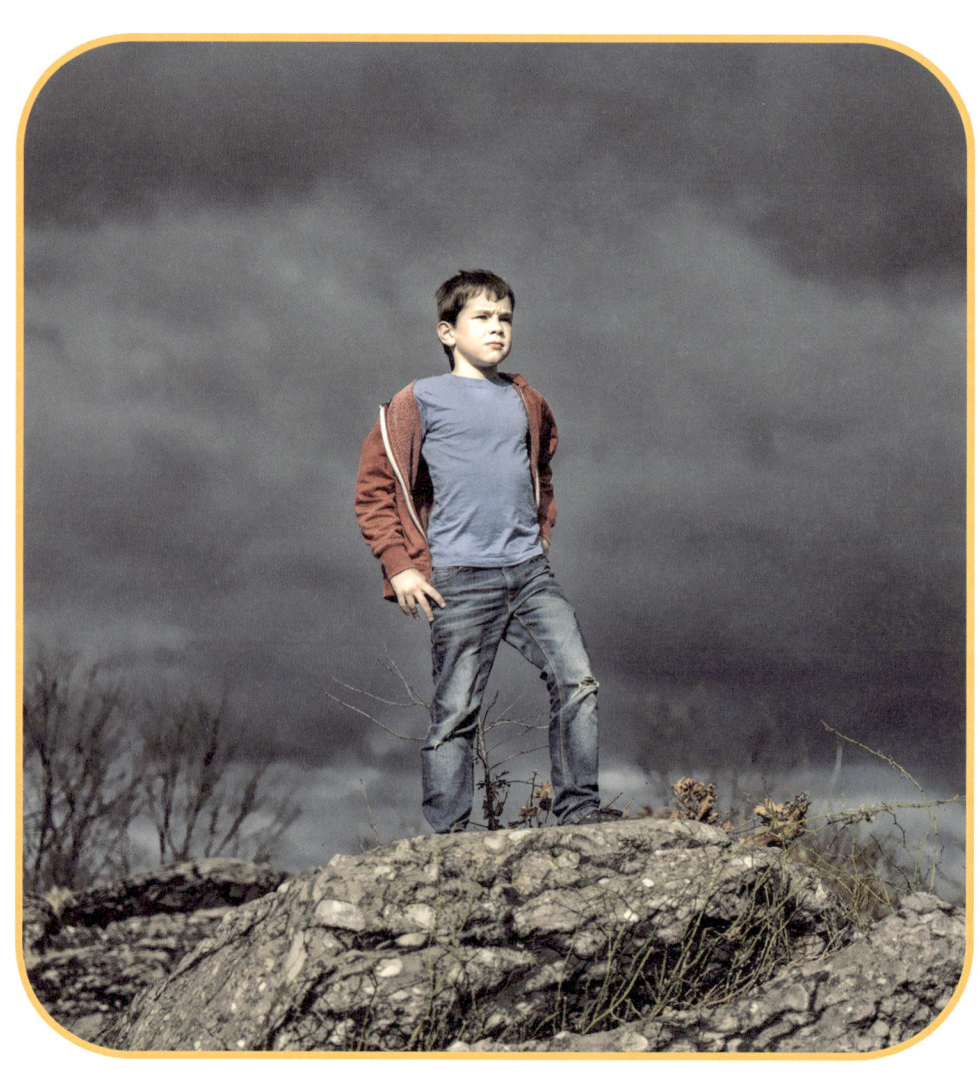

cloudy

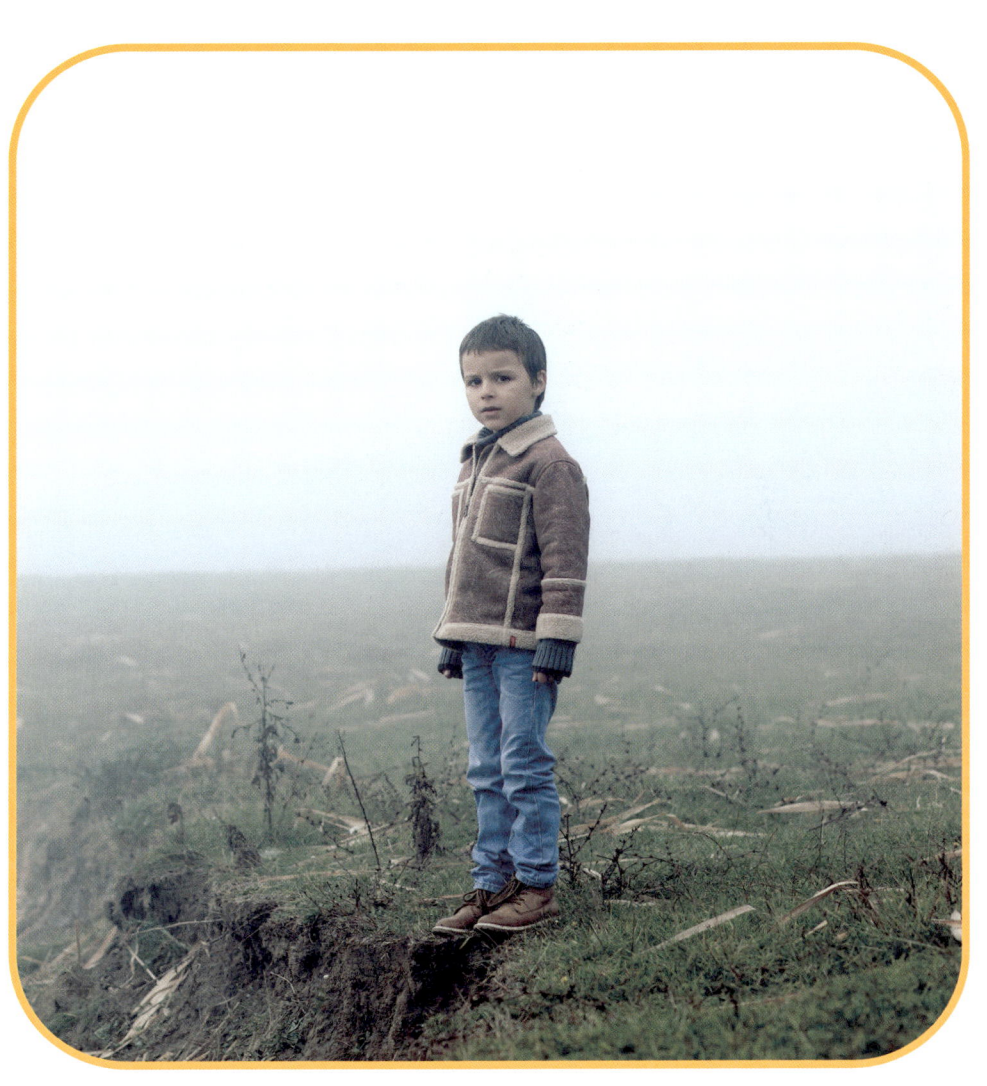

foggy

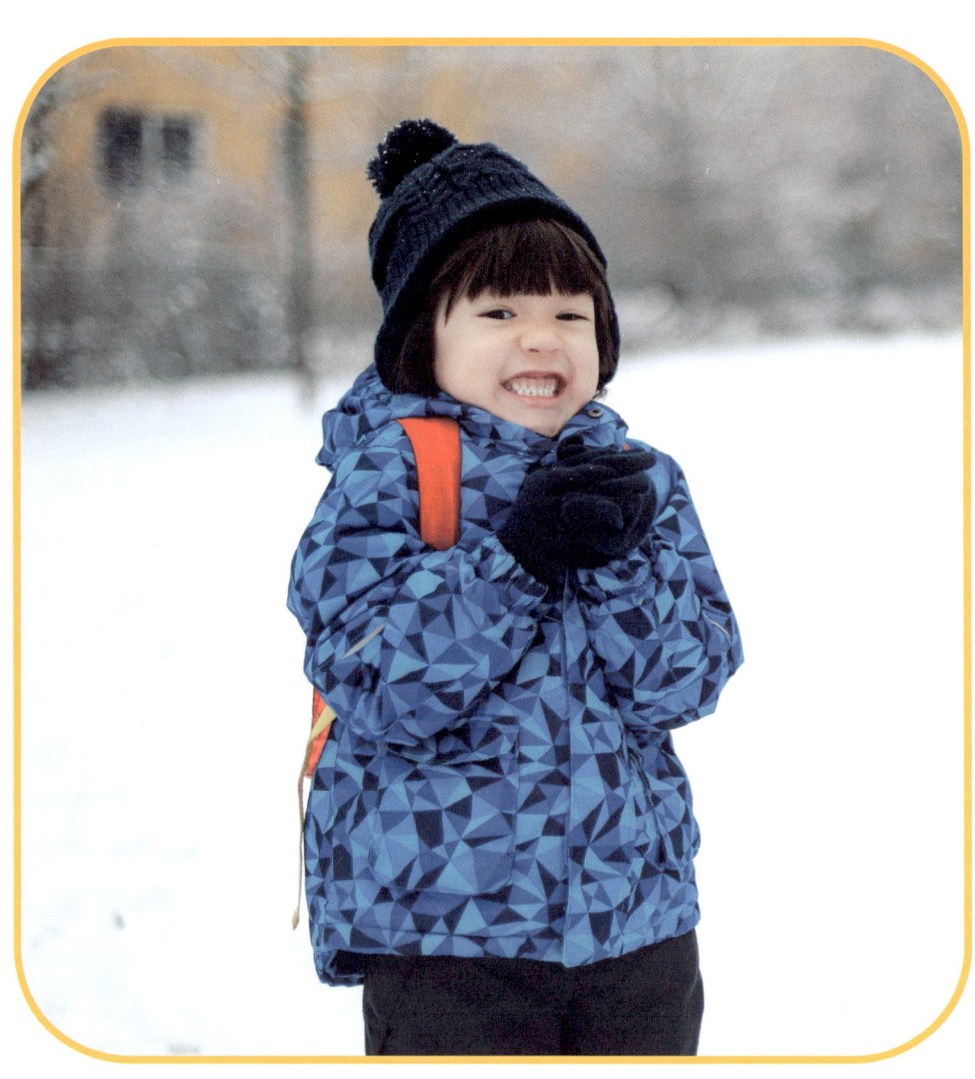

cold

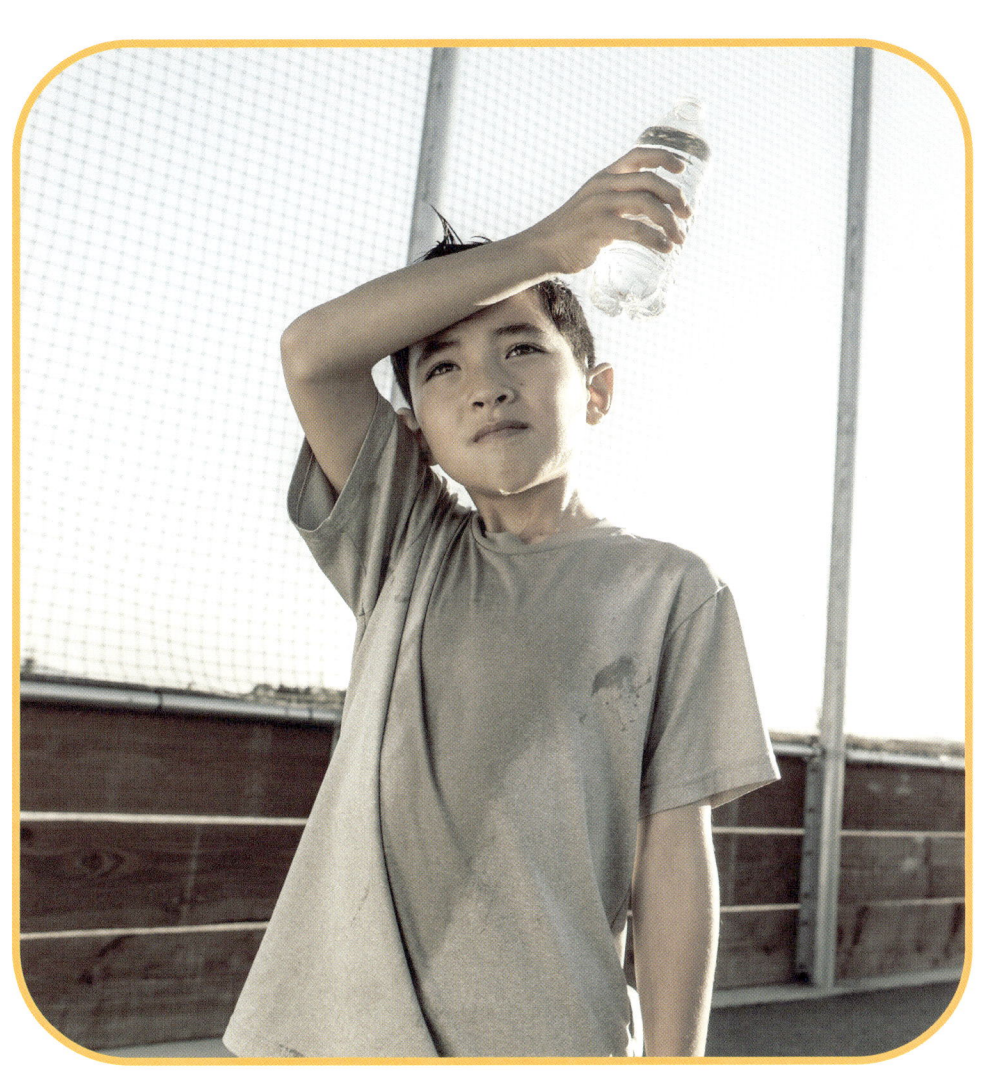

hot

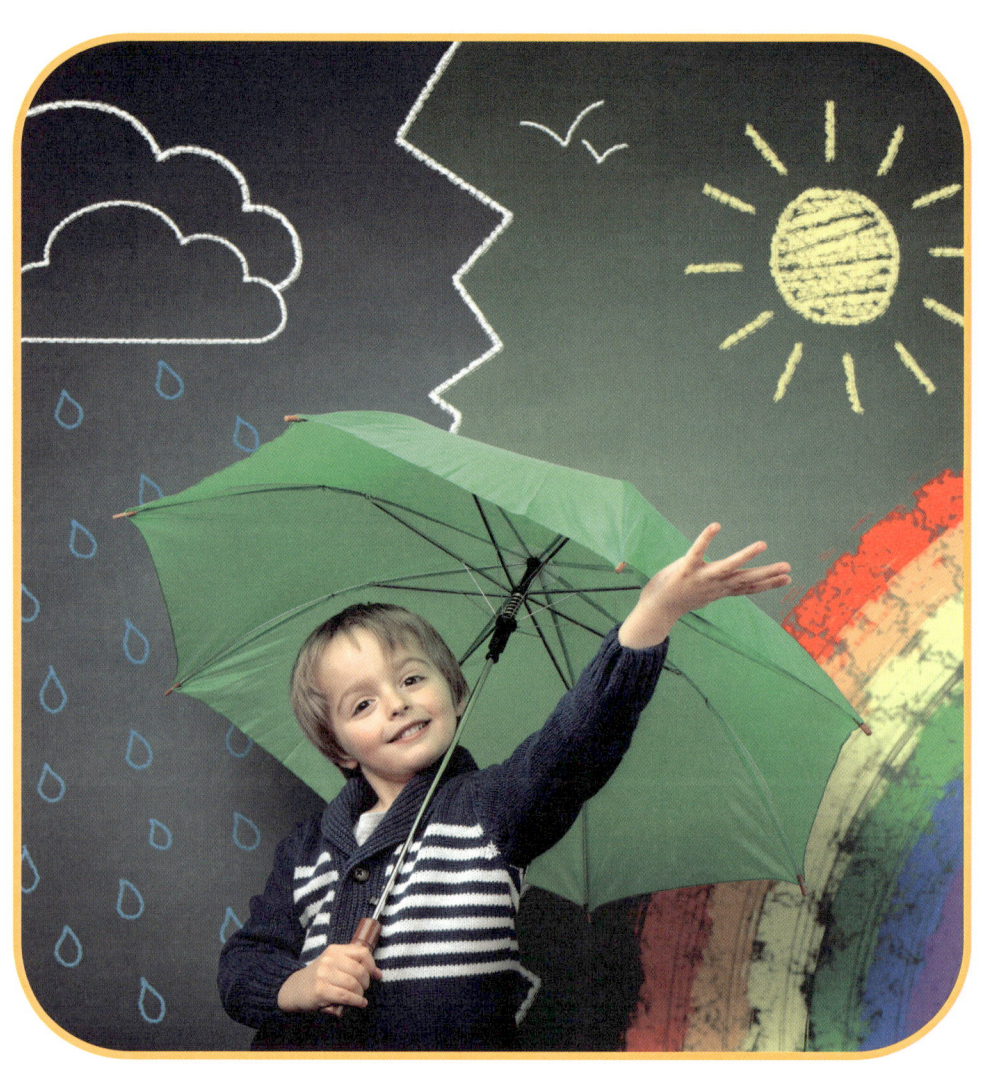

How's the weather?

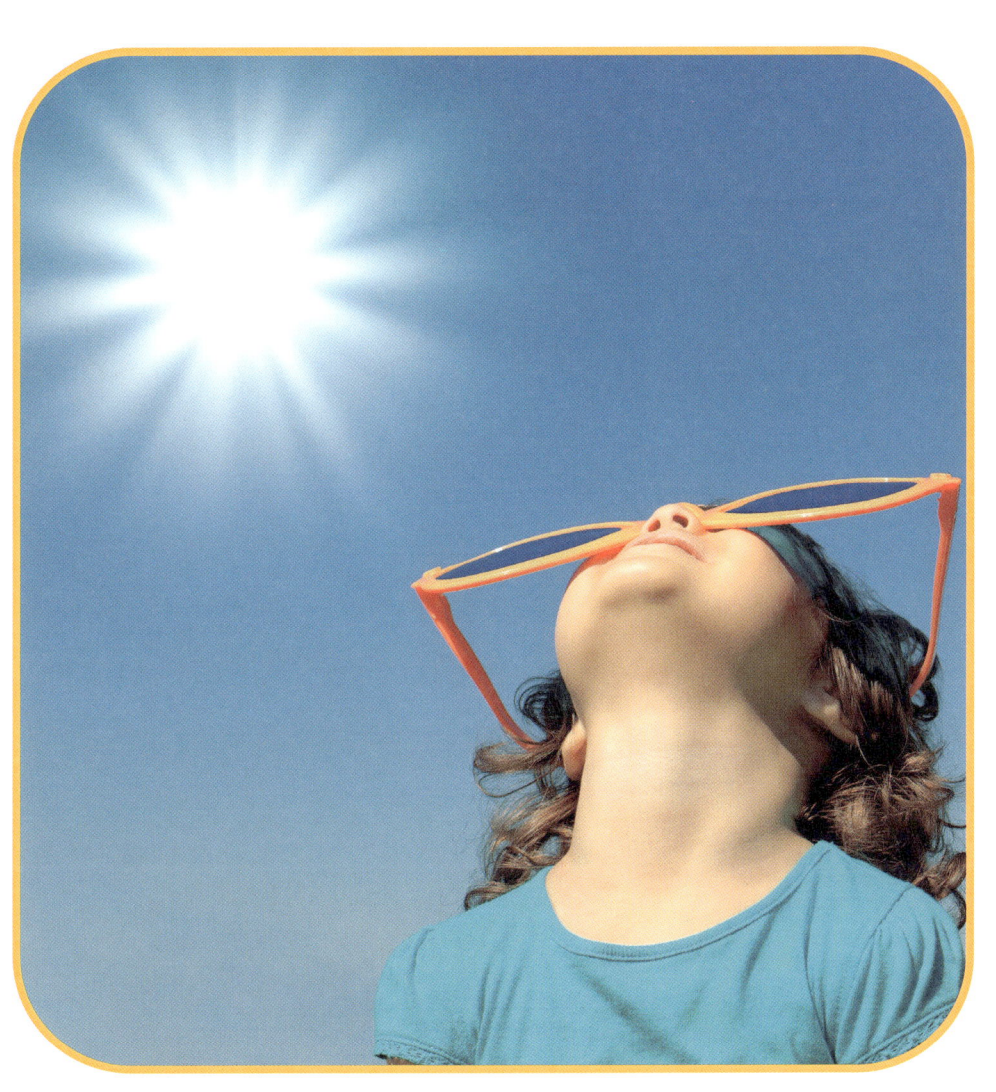

It's sunny.

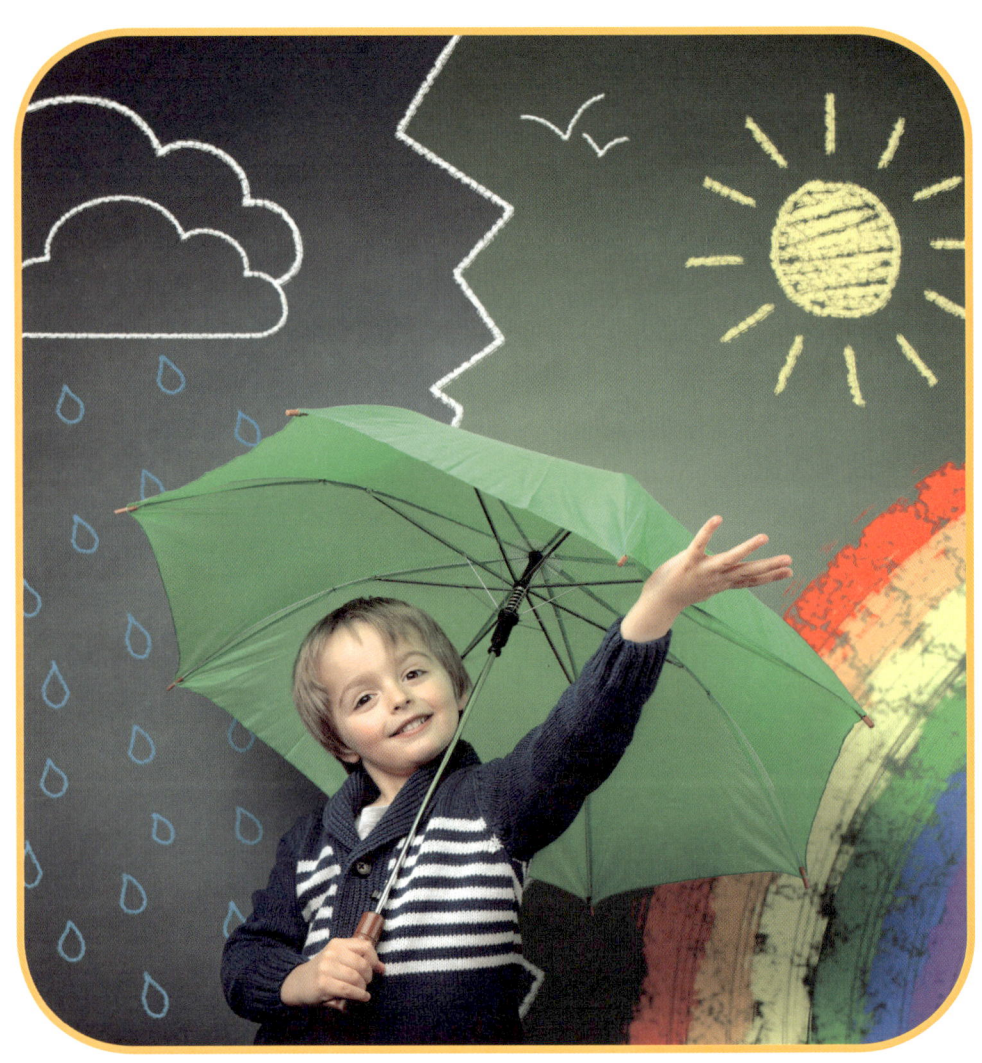

How's the weather?

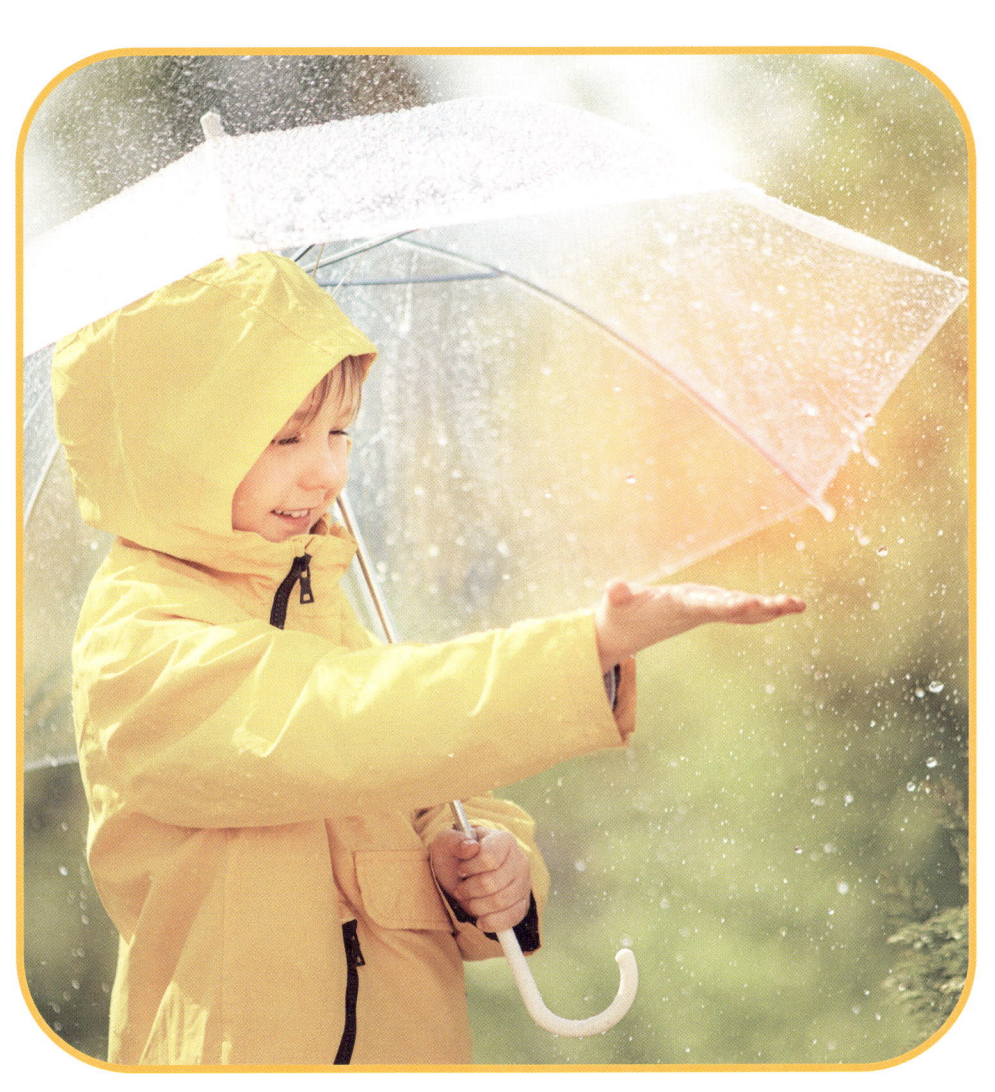

It's rainy.

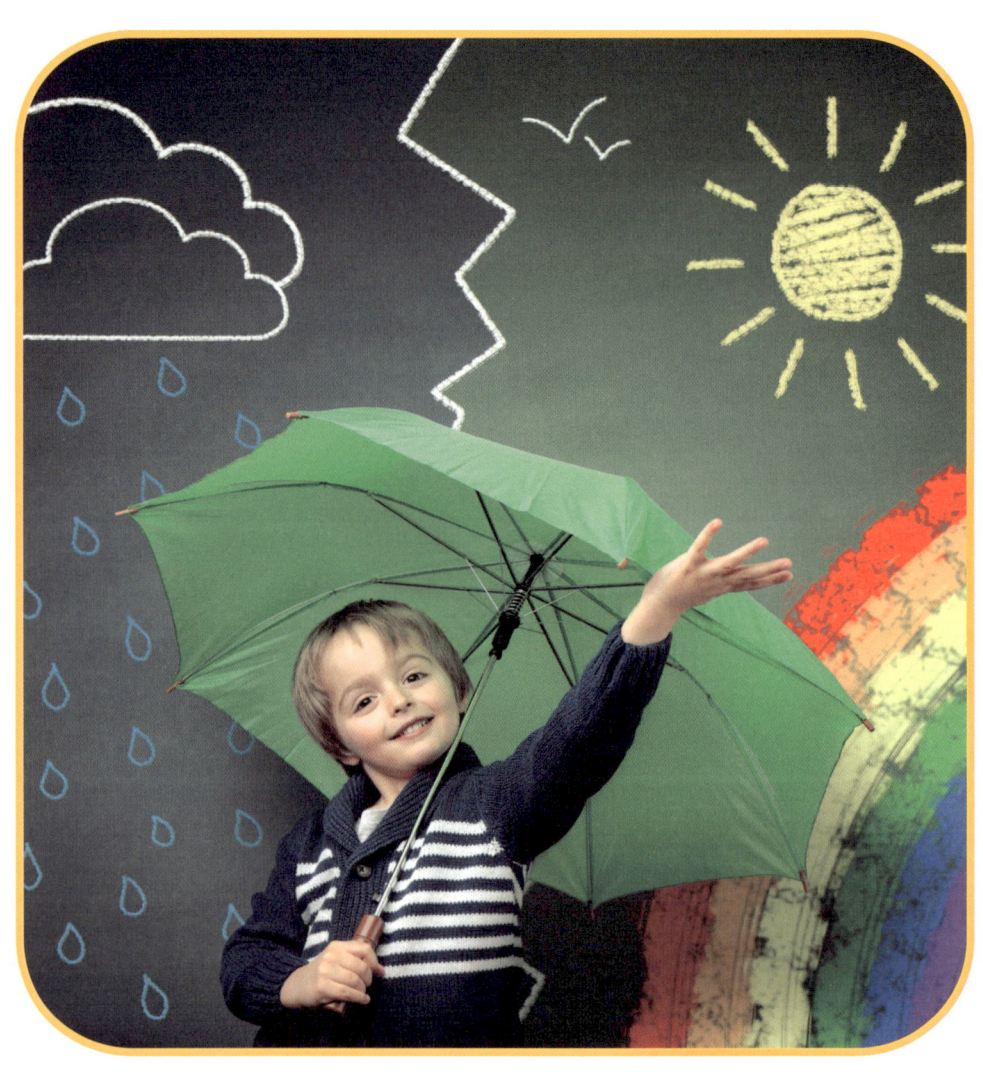

How's the weather?

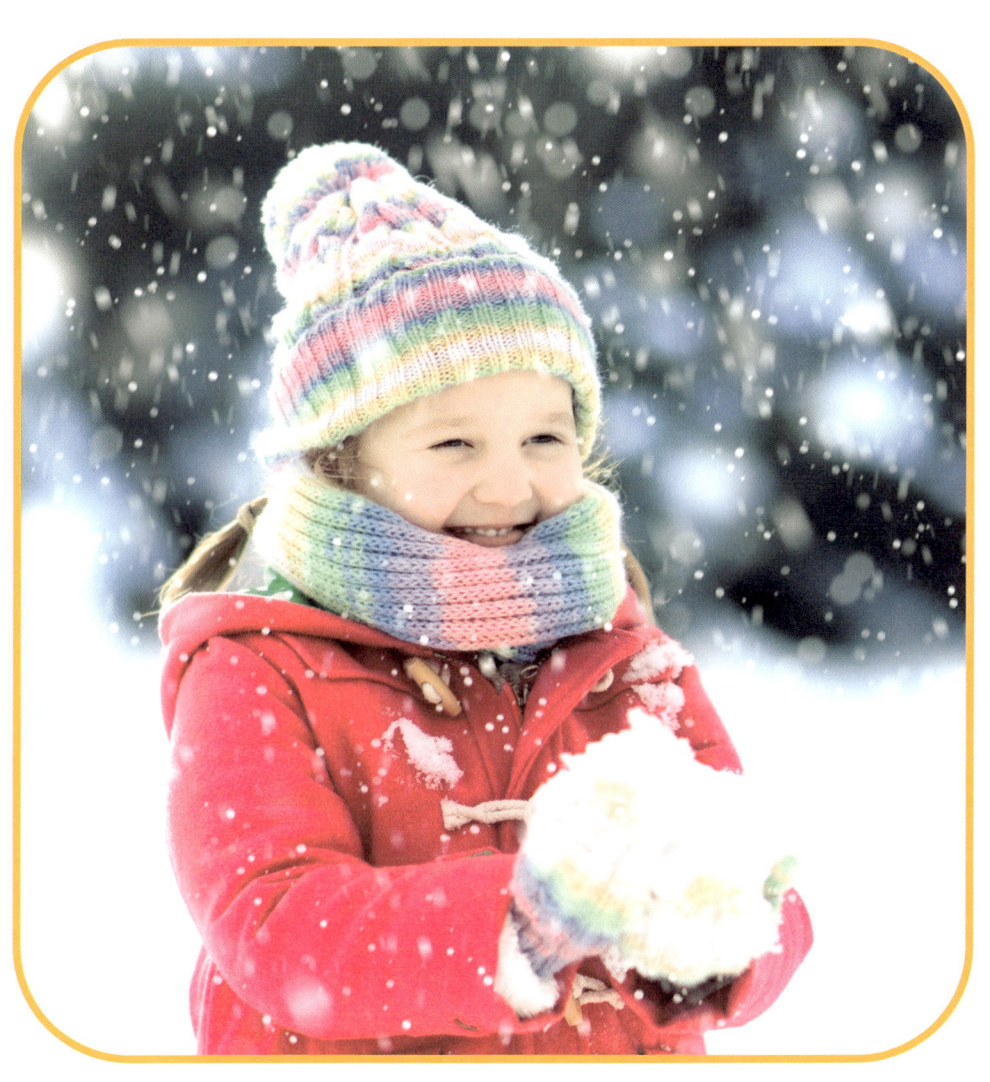

It's snowy.

Word List

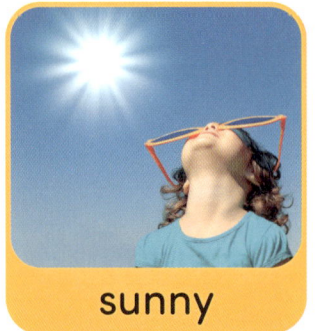

sunny

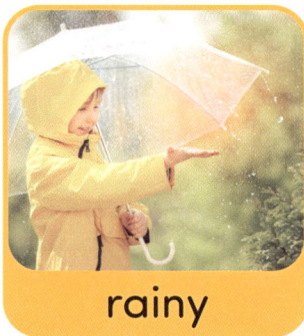

rainy

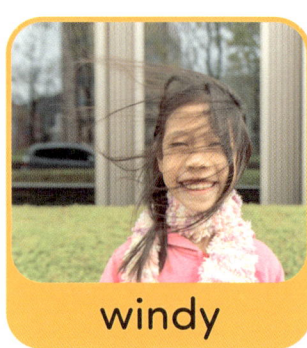

windy

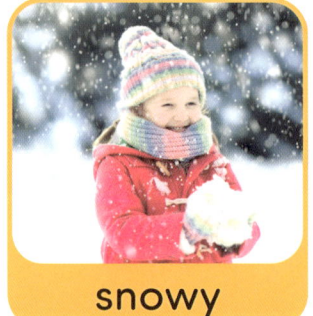

snowy

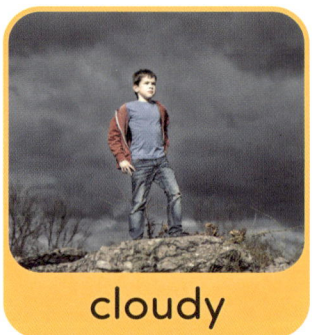

cloudy

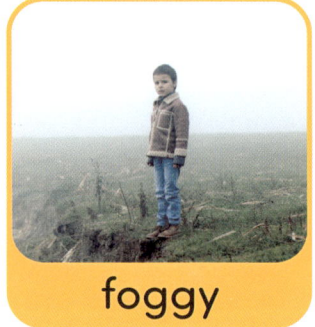

foggy

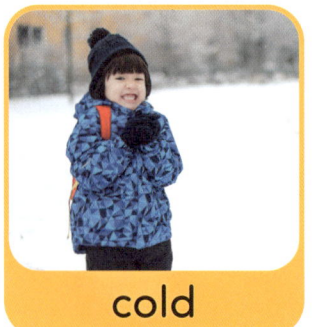

cold

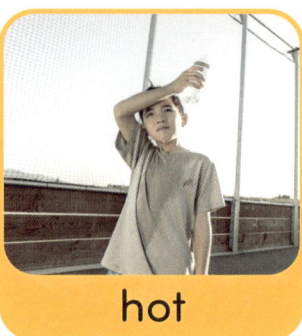

hot